Welcome Gospel Story for Kids!

The Bible is one great big story—the gospel story! From beginning to end, it's the good news of Jesus and how he came to save those who love him. All the people in the Bible and all their stories fit together to tell that good news.

The gospel story begins at the beginning, of course, with God's good creation and Adam and Eve. As you dive into these stories from God's Word, you won't just learn facts. You'll learn truths that transform you. They will change the way you see yourself, the way you treat others, and the way you love God. And they will help you become everything God created you to be and do everything he asks you to do.

In these pages, you will . . .

- discover **True Tales of Transformed People**, including Noah, Abraham and Sarah, Joseph, Ruth, and Esther—ordinary people like you—and see how God changed their lives and the world around them forever;
- find out what crowns and a moldy sandwich have to do with memorizing God's Word in the **Key Verse Challenge**;
- decide what you would do in real-life situations in **Choose to Change**;
- learn how to apply the Bible to your life and share it with others in **Know, Grow, and Go**;
- uncover fascinating **Factoids** about Joseph's sons, the diversity of God's people, Mary Magdalene, and more;
- dive deep into the details of prophecies, Jesus' family tree, and Passover—and learn why they matter—in **Big Ideas of the Bible**;
- search for King Xerxes's treasure in a **Seek and Find** challenge;
- follow the **map** to journey along with Jesus in his ministry;
- and even learn how to tell others about all that Jesus did and how they can love and trust him too!

So . . . are you ready to dive in? Are you ready to be transformed? Then let's go!

Visit Tyndale's website for kids at tyndale.com/kids.

Tyndale is a registered trademark of Tyndale House Ministries. The Tyndale Kids logo is a trademark of Tyndale House Ministries.

The Gospel Story for Kids: God's Story of Love from Creation to Revelation

Copyright © 2024 by Tyndale House Ministries. All rights reserved.

Illustrations copyright © Sarah Demonteverde. All rights reserved.

Designed by Jacqueline L. Nuñez

Scripture quotations are taken from the *Holy Bible*, New Living Translation, copyright © 1996, 2004, 2015 by Tyndale House Foundation. Used by permission of Tyndale House Publishers, Carol Stream, Illinois 60188. All rights reserved.

For manufacturing information regarding this product, please call 1-855-277-9400.

For information about special discounts for bulk purchases, please contact Tyndale House Publishers at csresponse@tyndale.com, or call 1-855-277-9400.

Library of Congress Cataloging-in-Publication Data

A catalog record for this book is available from the Library of Congress.

ISBN 979-8-4005-0131-9

Printed in China

30	29	28	27	26	25	24
7	6	5	4	3	2	1

Diving into the Story

Have you ever wondered how to discover what a Bible story is all about? It's not as hard as it might seem. Here's the secret: to understand a story, don't look just at what *happens* but at what *changes*.

Some Bible stories are about how people change. Other stories are about how God changes the world in big or small ways. Bible stories show us what God was doing in the past, and God still transforms people through these stories today.

Stories aren't just lists of things that happen; they're about people hoping to accomplish or avoid something. When you read a Bible story, look for God and how he changes people's lives. No matter which Bible story you're reading, ask these four questions:

1. Who struggles?
2. What do they discover?
3. How do things change?
4. What can I learn about God and myself from this story?

God's Good Creation

God made the entire universe out of nothing. He transformed empty darkness into a place full of life that shows us how powerful, creative, and loving he is.

We learn in Genesis that God created the concept of time by separating days from nights. He created the sun, moon, and stars that shine on us. He created the sturdy ground that we walk on and the trees and flowers that grow out of it. God created all the fascinating creatures that swim in the seas, fly in the sky, and walk on the earth. And, most importantly, God created Adam and Eve, the first humans, and gave them a beautiful place to live called Eden.

Eden was filled with different kinds of plants, including the tree of life and the tree of the knowledge of good and evil. God told Adam and Eve that they could eat fruit from every tree except one. Only the tree of the knowledge of good and evil was off limits. Unfortunately, Adam and Eve disobeyed God's command. As a consequence, they could not live in the garden with him anymore.

But—spoiler alert! God did not give up on the people he had made. He had a plan that would transform their hearts and bring them back to live in a glorious new home with him. Just like the Garden of Eden, this new home will have a tree of life, and the tree of life will bring joy and healing to all who believe in Jesus. What good news!

Adam and Eve Disobey God

God gave Adam and Eve only one rule in the Garden of Eden: don't eat fruit from the tree of the knowledge of good and evil. Satan, the enemy of God, knew this rule too. But he wanted to trick Adam and Eve into disobeying God.

He appeared as a talking snake and asked Eve, "Did God *really* say you can't eat any fruit in the garden?"

"Of course not!" Eve said. "There's only one tree we can't eat from. If we eat its fruit or even touch it, we'll die."

"You won't die," that sneaky old snake lied. "But you will be like God."

Satan and his lies tempted Adam and Eve to do much more than eat a piece of fruit. He tempted them to question what God said. And he tempted them to wonder if *their* way was better than *God's* way.

Those lies and tricks worked so well on Adam and Eve that Satan still uses them to tempt you today. He wants you to wonder, *Did God really say that?* And he wants you to say, "Maybe *my* way is better than *God's* way."

The good news is that God doesn't leave you to face Satan's temptations all on your own! He's given you his words in the Bible so you can know exactly what he says. God also invites you to pray and ask him for help. And best of all, God promises to give you everything you need to choose what's right and say no to Satan's sneaky lies (see Proverbs 3:5-6)!

CHOOSE TO CHANGE Read Genesis 3:1-19.

The man blamed God for making the woman who gave him the forbidden fruit to eat. What would you do if you got caught eating cookies meant for a classroom party?

A. Tell the teacher to stop putting cookies where you can reach them.

B. Apologize and stop eating the cookies.

C. Yell at the baker for making the cookies too yummy.

Answer: B, because it's best to tell the truth and take responsibility when you do something wrong.

Noah and the Flood

Know, Grow, and Go
God's Great Plan
Read Genesis 8:15–9:17.

When the world's people became so evil they couldn't even think about anything else, God was deeply hurt (Genesis 6:6). He could have walked away forever. Instead, God blessed Noah, his family, and the animals with a new beginning. Yet even as God painted that first rainbow, he knew people would do evil things again. God already had a solution though—not to destroy the world, but to save his people forever. Noah's story points toward the New Testament, when Jesus would come to rescue people from sin! The next time you see a rainbow, thank God for his great plan.

When God made Adam and Eve leave the garden, that wasn't the end of their story.

Adam and Eve had children who grew up to have children of their own—and those children grew up to have even more children. Hundreds of years passed, and many, many people lived on the earth.

But the people forgot God. They chose to do and say and think evil things *all the time*! God was sorry he had made them, and he decided to destroy them all with a flood.

Except Noah.

Noah loved God. So God told him to build a boat. A huge boat! And he told Noah *exactly* how to build it.

So what did Noah do? He started building.

It was hard work, and it took years and years! Noah's neighbors probably laughed and thought he had lost his mind. *Why would anyone build such a huge boat? And who needs so many animals?*

But Noah kept building—just as God told him to do. At last, the boat was finished. Noah, his family, and every kind of animal on earth climbed aboard. When the rains fell and the waters covered the land, God kept them all safe inside the boat. God used Noah and that boat to give the earth and his people a whole new beginning. He put a rainbow in the sky as a sign of his promise never to flood the earth again.

Obeying God won't always be easy, but it will always be the right choice. Because God takes care of those who love him.

Abraham and Sarah

IN A SNAPSHOT
- Lived as foreigners in Egypt
- Waited twenty-five years for a son
- Ancestors of the people of Israel
- Remembered for their faith

Big Promises: God called Abraham and Sarah—originally named Abram and Sarai—to leave their country and family and go to an unknown land. How would you feel if God asked you to move away from everything you knew? God promised they would become a great nation, possess a lot of land, and have more people in their family than they could count! There was one big problem though: they were way past the age when people can usually have babies. But they believed God could do what he said.

Bad Decisions: Abram and Sarai's lives were like a roller coaster—up with hope, down with doubt. While they lived in Egypt, Abram pretended Sarai was his sister, not his wife, because he thought the lie would make things easier for them. Then Sarai got tired of waiting for a son, so she came up with an idea: get Abram to marry their servant Hagar and have a child with her instead. They couldn't understand how God was going to do something they'd never seen before.

Impossible to Incredible: God gave the couple new names to prepare for their great blessing: Abraham and Sarah. These names were a sign of how God was doing something new through them. Finally, after twenty-five years, their promised son was born! It was so incredible, they laughed with joy. They even named their son Isaac, which means "laughter."

Abraham and Sarah's descendants became the people of Israel. Eventually, Jesus was born into Abraham's family too. Abraham had doubts and made mistakes, but God transformed his heart and life. Abraham trusted God, and God kept his promise.

PASS THE TESTS
Think of the last test or quiz you took. Abraham faced a number of tests in his life, but they were a lot different from the tests you take in school. He was far from perfect, but he trusted God, even when God tested him.

Can you remember a time when it was hard for you to have faith in God? Today, pray that God would strengthen your faith and remind you how trustworthy he is.

Jacob and Esau

Abraham and Sarah's son, Isaac, grew up and married Rebekah. God blessed them with twin boys. But those boys fought right from the start—even before they were born! Esau was the oldest and his father's favorite, but Rebekah loved Jacob best.

Jacob grew up to be a trickster. With Rebekah's help, he even tricked his father into giving him Esau's blessing. This was a terrible trick! Esau was so angry that he wanted to kill Jacob.

To escape, Jacob ran far away to his uncle Laban's land. There, he fell in love with Rachel, but the trickster was tricked into marrying her sister, Leah, instead. Later, Jacob married Rachel too, and their family and riches grew. One day, God told Jacob to gather his family and go back to his father's land. Jacob obeyed, but he wondered if Esau still wanted to kill him. So when he heard that Esau was riding out to meet him with an army of 400 men, Jacob was terrified!

Hoping to make Esau less angry, Jacob sent gifts of goats, camels, cows, donkeys, and more. When the two brothers met at last, Jacob bowed down to Esau *seven times*. But Esau ran toward him and . . . hugged him! Esau's heart had changed. He had forgiven his brother, and they lived together in their father's land in peace.

Jacob—who was also called Israel—had twelve sons. But like his own father, Jacob had a favorite, and his name was Joseph.

True Story
Joseph and his wife—who was Egyptian—had two sons. Their names were Manasseh and Ephraim, and they were born in the land of Egypt. Before Joseph's father died, he blessed each of the boys by placing his hands on top of their heads. This showed his love for them. Did you know that God loves everyone the same and purposely chose to include people from different ethnic backgrounds in Joseph's family tree? It's true!

FACTOID!

Joseph

IN A SNAPSHOT

- Had eleven brothers and one sister
- Sold into slavery
- Accused of a crime he didn't commit
- Became a leader of Egypt

Sibling Rivalry: Joseph was the favorite child, and he knew it! What's more, he flaunted it in front of his older brothers. Things just got worse when his father, Jacob, gave him a fancy, colorful new coat—and didn't give anything to his brothers. And guess what Joseph did when he had a dream about his brothers bowing down to him? That's right—he told them all about it. How would you feel if you were one of Joseph's brothers? The brothers couldn't take much more of Joseph's arrogance. One day, they tore off Joseph's new coat, tossed him in a pit, and sold him into slavery (kind of an extreme reaction, even if Joseph was annoying).

Second Chances: God wasn't done with Joseph yet! God gave him a second chance to learn from this experience and do the right thing. Instead of giving in to despair, Joseph worked hard and did his best with the situation he was in. When he was falsely accused of a crime and thrown into prison, he could have gotten angry at God and turned his back on him. But he didn't! God still had a plan for Joseph—and years later, God even paved the way for him to become an important leader in Egypt.

A Great Leader: Joseph's God-given leadership ability helped him guide the people of Egypt through a terrible famine. When his brothers came to him begging for food, they didn't recognize him at first. This could have been Joseph's moment to get revenge! But God had changed Joseph's heart since he was an immature kid showing off in front of his brothers. He chose to give them food and forgive them for what they'd done to him. Joseph had become wise enough to recognize that God was at work in his life all along, especially in the most difficult times.

DREAM ON

In Bible times, God often used dreams to talk to his people—and some of those dreams were pretty strange too.

How many special dreams can you find in Joseph's story?

CHOOSE TO FORGIVE . . . IT'S THE BEST WAY TO LIVE!

Joseph forgave his brothers even though they had done horrible things to him. Can you think of someone you need to forgive? Why is forgiveness such a big deal to God?

Moses and the Ten Commandments

Joseph's entire family moved to Egypt and became known as the Israelites. Years passed, and a new ruler came to power. He made the Israelites his slaves and had their baby boys thrown into the Nile River! Pharaoh's own daughter rescued one of the babies and named him Moses.

When Moses grew up, he angered Pharaoh and had to run far away. Years later, God called to Moses from a burning bush: "Go back to Egypt. Tell Pharaoh to let my people go."

Moses went, but Pharaoh wouldn't listen. It took ten terrible plagues to make Pharaoh let the Israelites go.

God led his people through the wilderness to Mount Sinai. There, he gave Moses ten commandments. These laws taught the Israelites how to love God and each other. And they helped the world see that the Israelites were God's chosen people.

One day, instead of giving them laws to follow, God would send his Holy Spirit to change their hearts forever with his love.

The Ten Commandments for Kids

1. Put God first in everything you do.
2. Worship God, and God only.
3. Honor God's name, and don't misuse it.
4. Set aside time for rest and prayer.
5. Respect and obey your parents.
6. Protect others and do not hate.
7. Be faithful to your husband or wife if you get married someday.
8. Don't steal.
9. Don't lie—tell the truth.
10. Be content, not jealous of what other people have.

Ruth and Naomi

IN A SNAPSHOT

- Lost their loved ones
- Traveled to Israel together
- Received help from Boaz
- Were blessed by God with a new family

From Bad to Worse: Naomi lived in Bethlehem with her husband and two sons. But a famine came, which means there wasn't enough food. So the family moved to the country of Moab. There, Naomi's husband died. Her sons married women named Ruth and Orpah, but after ten years, Naomi's sons both died too. Naomi was far from home with no family left. She was angry with God, and she didn't see how her life could ever be good again.

Return to Bethlehem: Naomi heard that crops were once again growing in Bethlehem, so she decided to return home. To her surprise, Ruth wanted to come too. Ruth said, "Don't ask me to leave you and turn back. Wherever you go, I will go; wherever you live, I will live. Your people will be my people, and your God will be my God" (Ruth 1:16). So Naomi let Ruth join her on her journey home. By the time Ruth arrived in Israel, she had committed to worship and serve God. But it was tough to fit in in a new place.

A New Home: Ruth wasn't just ordinary. In her world, she was *less* than ordinary. Not only was she from a far-off land, but she was also a widow, and she had no money. Ruth survived and helped her mother-in-law, Naomi, by picking up the leftover grain dropped in someone else's field.

Ruth may not have had riches or fancy things, but she did have faith. She chose to trust and follow the God whom Naomi had told her about. And God used that faith and trust to do *extraordinary* things.

A Bright Future: God took that poor, out-of-place, less-than-ordinary woman and completely transformed her life. Remember that field Ruth worked in? It was owned by a man named Boaz, and he became Ruth's husband. Then God blessed them with a son. And he didn't stop there. God made Ruth part of his own family! She became the great-grandmother of King David and the great-great-great-*whole-bunch-of-greats!*-grandmother of Jesus.

All because she loved and trusted and followed God.

That's what God does. He takes ordinary (and less-than-ordinary) people who choose to love and trust and follow him, and he does extraordinary things in their lives. He did it for Ruth and King David, for Moses and Mary, for Peter and Paul, and for so many others in the Bible.

God's not finished! He is still doing extraordinary things in the lives of ordinary people. And guess what? When you choose to love and trust and follow him, he will do extraordinary things in your life too.

Know, Grow, and Go
All Part of the Plan *Read Ruth 2.*

Out of all the fields in Bethlehem, Ruth *just so happened* to choose Boaz's field. And Boaz *just so happened* to be Naomi's relative. Some people call that a *coincidence*. That's when two or more things happen at the same time by accident. The thing is, nothing God does is by accident. God is so amazing that he uses even our ordinary choices as part of his great plan. We can trust him with the smallest details of our lives.

Samuel Anoints David

God had big plans for Ruth's great-grandson David. At this time, Israel's first king, Saul, did whatever he thought was right, even if God said it was wrong. So God decided it was time to choose a new king.

God sent his prophet Samuel to Bethlehem to find a descendant of Ruth named Jesse. God would choose one of his sons to be Israel's new king.

Samuel found Jesse and asked him to call all his sons together. He took one look at Jesse's oldest son, Eliab, and thought, *This must be the new king! He looks so tall and strong, just like a king should look.*

But God said, "No. He's not the new king."

God didn't care how his new king looked on the outside. He cared about what was on the inside—what the king thought about, how he helped others, and most of all, how he loved and followed God.

So God said no to Jesse's sons—all except the youngest one, David, who was still out in the fields taking care of the sheep. When David was finally brought to Samuel, God said, "That's him! He's the one!"

David had a heart that loved God. And that's exactly the kind of heart God wants you to have too.

> **Don't judge by his appearance or height, for I have rejected him. The LORD doesn't see things the way you see them. People judge by outward appearance, but the LORD looks at the heart.**
>
> **1 Samuel 16:7**

Key Verse Challenge
1 SAMUEL 16:7
What if you got a present wrapped in fancy paper and bows, but there was a moldy sandwich inside? Yuck! We usually notice the outside of a person first, but the inside is what matters most. Write this verse on a piece of paper, and list some of the inner qualities God wants us to have.

Esther

Who wrote it?
We don't know. Bible experts believe a Jewish writer who knew a lot about Persian history wrote it.

What's it about?
Beautiful palaces, secret identities, assassination plots, a foiled plan to kill thousands, and triumphant parades. This important part of Jewish history starts with King Xerxes of Persia throwing a massive party. During the celebration, Queen Vashti refuses the king's request. That's when the beautiful Esther enters the story. She becomes the next queen but hides the fact that she's Jewish. When evil Haman comes up with a plan to kill Esther's people, Esther risks her life to stop him. Even though God's name is not mentioned, it's clear that he is at work in everything that happens in this book.

Where does it take place?
The events of this book happen in the land of Persia—mainly in the capital city of Susa.

When does it take place?
The story of Esther takes place from around 483 to 473 BC.

Why does this book matter?
Throughout history, God raises up the right person at the right time in the right place. Esther is a perfect example. She is able to save her people because God works out events so she can become queen. We should never forget that God calls each of us to follow him in special ways. He's put us in our homes, churches, and schools so we can love and serve others in those places.

How does it fit in God's story?
God is always at work helping and saving his people. The book of Esther is a reminder that nothing is outside his control. Even events that seem hopeless can be used by God for good. This is just as true now as it was in Esther's time!

SEEK AND FIND
King Xerxes built great wealth and power by expanding the Persian Empire with many wars. Look for these signs of his wealth in the book of Esther:

1. A party that lasts nearly six months
2. A signet ring
3. Gold goblets with cool designs
4. A gold scepter

Timeline

483 BC:
King Xerxes banishes Queen Vashti.

479 BC:
Esther becomes queen of Persia.

Esther Saves Her People

Queen Esther knew something was terribly wrong. Her cousin Mordecai's clothes were ripped and torn, and he was weeping outside the palace. Esther sent a servant to find out why.

Mordecai sent a message back: A new law had been passed. The Jewish people—God's people—were going to be destroyed! Esther must help them. She *must* talk to the king.

But Esther had a problem: if she went to the king without being called, she could be killed herself. And King Xerxes hadn't called for her in a month.

Esther wanted to help, but it would take more courage than she had on her own. She asked the Jewish people to pray and fast, and she prayed and fasted too. *For three whole days.* Then Esther went to the king. Because she did, God's people were saved.

God's name doesn't appear in the book of Esther—not even one time. But he was there and working in every moment. God used Esther, Mordecai, and even King Xerxes to keep a promise. A promise that one day his people would return to their own land—the land where his Son, Jesus, would be born to be the Savior for all peoples.

Know, Grow, and Go
A Time to Be Brave *Read Esther 4.*

God has a plan for you. And there will come a time when he will ask you to be brave and do something for him. It might be standing up for others, telling the truth when it would be easier to lie, or doing right when everyone else is choosing wrong. Whatever God asks you to do, you can be sure he'll be right there helping you be brave.

Prophecy 101

In Esther's story, God rescued the Jews from harm. As many years passed, God's people were conquered by other enemies, including the Romans. But God promised to save them one day. He sent special messages about things that will happen in the future. These are called prophecies, and someone who shares prophecies from God is called a prophet.

One way we know the Bible is the Word of God is that there are hundreds of fulfilled prophecies, meaning those predictions from God's prophets came true. And a whole bunch of these prophecies point toward Jesus!

Here are just a few amazing prophecies about Jesus, along with their fulfillment in the New Testament:

- Isaiah prophesied that "a great light" would come to Galilee and extend to the whole nation of Israel. (See Isaiah 9:1-3 and Matthew 4:12-17.)

- Micah prophesied that a great ruler would be born in Bethlehem—and his prophecy was over 400 years before Jesus' birth! (See Micah 5:2 and Luke 2:4.)

- Zechariah prophesied that a "righteous" and "victorious" king would come to the people of Jerusalem, but he would be "riding on a donkey's colt." (See Zechariah 9:9 and John 12:12-15.)

Key Figures in Jesus' Genealogy

A genealogy is a list of people in a family, sometimes going back hundreds or thousands of years. For instance, your genealogy would include you, your parents, your grandparents, your great-grandparents, and on and on. The Bible features a lot of genealogies, and sometimes they just seem like boring lists of names. But they're there for a reason! The genealogy of Jesus in Matthew 1 shows that Jesus' ancestors included Abraham and David. Matthew wanted his readers to understand that Jesus was the King and Savior descended from David that the Old Testament speaks about. Read on for some of the other important people in Jesus' genealogy.

Abraham was chosen by God to be the father of God's people, the Israelites.

Isaac was the son of Abraham and his wife, Sarah. He was the first of the many descendants God promised to Abraham.

Jacob's sons and their families became the twelve tribes of Israel. God did incredible things for Jacob's family, including setting them free from slavery in Egypt.

Rahab was a woman who lived a sinful lifestyle, but she saved the lives of two Israelite spies and became part of God's family.

Ruth was a courageous woman who was faithful to her mother-in-law after both their husbands died. Like Rahab, she wasn't an Israelite, but God brought her into his family.

David is considered the greatest king of Israel. God promised his family would rule Israel forever (2 Samuel 7:16), a promise that pointed ahead to Jesus.

Mary became Jesus' mother when she was a young woman. She is the only person in the genealogy who was with Jesus throughout his earthly life.

The Birth of Jesus

One day, when the time was just right, God sent the angel Gabriel to the village of Nazareth. He had a message for a young girl named Mary. That message would change the whole world!

"The Lord is with you, Mary!" Gabriel said. "You're going to have a baby, and he will be the Son of God!"

"How is that possible?" Mary asked. She was engaged to Joseph, but they were not yet married.

"God's words always come true!" Gabriel said.

When Joseph discovered that Mary was going to have a baby, he didn't understand. But an angel came and said, "Don't be afraid to take Mary as your wife. Her baby is from God." So Joseph did just as the angel said.

When it was almost time for Mary's baby to be born, the Roman emperor ordered everyone to return to their hometown to be counted. So Joseph and Mary set out on the long journey to Bethlehem.

In Bethlehem, the inn was full. Mary and Joseph found shelter in a stable with the animals. And there, Mary had her baby. They named him Jesus. Mary wrapped him in soft, snuggly cloths and laid in him a manger.

> **Key Verse Challenge**
> ISAIAH 9:6
> Make a crown out of construction paper and write the titles listed in these verses around the crown. Then memorize the verses one line at a time. This is just one of many prophecies in Isaiah that points ahead to the Messiah, Jesus.

That night, an angel appeared to some shepherds in the fields. He said, "The Savior has been born today in Bethlehem! You'll find him wrapped in cloths and lying in a manger."

The shepherds ran to Bethlehem. They found Mary and Joseph and the baby in the manger. And they told everyone about all that the angel had said: the Savior—the Messiah—had been born!

> A child is born to us,
>   a son is given to us.
> The government will rest on his shoulders.
>   And he will be called:
> Wonderful Counselor, Mighty God,
>   Everlasting Father, Prince of Peace.
>
>   Isaiah 9:6

Jesus' Life

Jesus was born in Bethlehem (see Matthew 1:18–2:6; Luke 2:1-7).

Jesus grew up wise and strong (see Luke 2:40).

Jesus died on the cross, taking the punishment for the world's sin (see John 19; Romans 6:23; 1 Corinthians 15:3).

Jesus rose from the dead (see Matthew 28; John 20)!

Jesus' Early Ministry

1. Jesus is born in Bethlehem.
2. When Herod dies, Joseph and Mary take Jesus to their home in Nazareth.
3. When he is twelve, Jesus visits Jerusalem with Joseph and Mary.
4. Jesus is almost thirty when he begins his public ministry. He is baptized in the Jordan River near Jericho.
5. Jesus' first miracle, turning water into wine, is performed in Cana in Galilee.
6. Jesus returns to Jerusalem, where he chases money changers from the Temple.
7. After a miraculous catch of fish on the Sea of Galilee, Jesus calls his first disciples.

Jesus' Last Supper

After three years of ministry, Jesus was almost finished with his mission on earth. It was the time of Passover, and he and his disciples gathered in Jerusalem to share the seder meal. It was the last meal they would eat together before Jesus went to the cross. Each food at the seder was a reminder of how God rescued the Israelites from slavery in Egypt.

Passover Lamb

Jesus celebrated the Passover—which reminds the Jewish people how God rescued them from Egypt—just like others before him had done for hundreds of years. The Passover festival included the sacrifice of a lamb. Jesus is known as the Lamb of God, and he sacrificed himself for our sins just a few days after celebrating Passover. This timing was no accident—it was all part of God's amazing plan.

Roasted lamb reminded them of the lamb God told those long-ago Israelites to sacrifice. Vegetables were a symbol of the hyssop used to paint the lamb's blood over their doorways so the plague of death would "pass over" them. Unleavened bread was a reminder of how the bread had no time to rise as the Israelites hurried out of Egypt. Bitter herbs represented the bitterness of slavery and of not being able to worship God. Charoseth (a mixture of apples, pears, nuts, and wine) was like the mortar the slaves used to build cities of brick for the Egyptians. Eggs were a symbol of their sadness, while wine represented all that God did to save the Israelites from slavery.

But when Jesus died on the cross and rose again, he forever changed the meaning of the seder meal. Today, we can still share a seder meal to celebrate Passover. But it isn't just to celebrate the Israelites' freedom from slavery. Jesus transformed it into a celebration of the freedom he offers to all people—freedom from sin and death and freedom to live a rich and wonderful life with him forever.

Seder: A Passover Celebration

The seder is a special meal held during Passover, which is a Jewish festival that celebrates the Israelites' freedom from slavery in Egypt. The seder meal is typically held on the first or second night of Passover. This traditional holiday meal starts with songs and readings about the Passover story. Although the foods on a seder table can vary, here's what a traditional seder meal might look like:

Jesus' Ultimate Sacrifice

After the Passover meal, Jesus and a few disciples went to pray in a nearby garden. All of a sudden, the religious leaders who hated Jesus came charging in. They brought soldiers and torches and weapons, and they arrested Jesus. All because Jesus' disciple Judas betrayed him and told his enemies where to find him. The other disciples ran off, leaving Jesus to be taken away alone.

The soldiers tied Jesus up and took him to the high priest for a trial. But it wasn't a fair trial. The officials had already decided Jesus had to die because they didn't believe that he was the Son of God. Townspeople told lies about him. He was slapped and beaten and spit upon.

Only the Romans could sentence a prisoner to death, so the religious leaders took Jesus to the Roman governor, Pilate. But Pilate couldn't find any reason to kill Jesus. He knew Jesus was a teacher who performed miracles. Why should he die? Pilate told the people they should let Jesus go free. But they shouted for his death on a cross: "Crucify him! Crucify him!"

Pilate turned Jesus over to his soldiers to be flogged—the most terrible kind of beating. The soldiers twisted thorns into a crown and forced it down on his head. They laughed as they called him the King of the Jews. What kind of king lets himself get beat up by soldiers?

Again, Pilate tried to free Jesus, but the crowds only shouted louder, "Crucify him! Crucify him!" So Pilate sentenced Jesus to die. Jesus was forced to drag his cross through town to a place outside the city walls. Soldiers nailed his hands and feet to the rough wooden cross.

With his last breath, Jesus said, "It is finished," and he died. The earth shook, the rocks split, and darkness covered the land. A Roman soldier at the cross said, "Surely he was the Son of God!"

For those who loved Jesus, it looked like the end of everything they had believed and hoped for. But in three days, all that would change!

Know, Grow, and Go
His Mission *Read John 19:28-30.*

"It is finished." Those were Jesus' last words before he died. But what was finished? *His mission to save us.* That mission started before the world began and continued throughout the Old Testament. Jesus' mission led him from heaven down to a manger in Bethlehem. And it ended when he died to take the punishment for the whole world's sins—and to open the doors of eternal life to everyone who believes in him.

Jesus' Resurrection

The disciples were heartbroken. They had believed Jesus would save them from all their enemies, but instead, he had died on the cross.

Two of Jesus' followers came and took his body off the cross. Because it was almost time for the Sabbath—the Jewish day of rest—they quickly wrapped him in spices and linen cloth. Then they placed him in a tomb carved into the rock. A huge stone was rolled over the entrance to seal his body inside, and Pilate sent soldiers to stand guard.

All that next day, Jesus' followers waited and wept. When the Sabbath ended, Mary Magdalene and some of the other women rose up early and went to the tomb. They wanted to finish preparing Jesus' body for burial. As they walked, they wondered who would help them roll that huge stone away.

But when they arrived at the tomb, the stone was already rolled away! An angel stood there, gleaming like lightning.

"Don't be afraid!" the angel said. "You are looking for Jesus, but he isn't here. He has risen just as he told you he would!"

The women ran back to tell the others the very best of news: Jesus was alive!

When God raised Jesus from death, everything changed. Not just for those women, and not just for the disciples. It changed everything for us too.

> **FACTOID**
>
> **Spreading the News**
> Did you know Mary Magdalene was the first person to see Jesus after he rose from the dead (see John 20:11-18)? During Bible times, women were viewed as less important than men, and their words weren't thought to be as reliable as what men said. But Jesus valued women and men equally. He gave Mary Magdalene a big job: spreading the news that he was alive!

Because Jesus is alive, we know the power of God is even stronger than death. In fact, it's stronger than anything we will ever face on this earth. And when we decide to love and follow Jesus, he pours that same power into our lives. Best of all, Jesus promises to be with us every moment of every day. He's always there to help us and to guide us—now and forever!

The Great Commission

Jesus loved each of us so much that he left heaven and came to this earth on a mission. That mission was to take the punishment for our sins, to defeat death, and to make a way for us to live with God forever. But that's not all Jesus came for. He also came to give his disciples a mission.

Just before Jesus returned to heaven, he gathered his disciples together one last time and said, "Go! Go and tell everyone about me. Baptize them in the name of the Father, Son, and Holy Spirit. Tell them everything I've taught you. Teach them how to live and how to love God."

That was Jesus' mission for his disciples. Not just Peter and Matthew and Mary. That's his mission for everyone who chooses to follow him, including you.

Jesus wants you to tell others about him and the good news he brings—whether that means talking to a big group or the kid next door. It's easy to share good news when you win a trophy or ace a test. So first ask yourself, Why do you think Jesus' story is good news for you?

If you are nervous about sharing this news, don't worry! God won't send you out on this mission alone. When you decide to follow Jesus, God sends his own Holy Spirit to live inside you. The Spirit will help you remember what God has said, and he'll help you have the courage to share it with others. He will also transform you from the inside out, making your heart, your words, and your actions more and more like Jesus.

 CHOOSE TO CHANGE Read Matthew 28:16-20.

How can you live out the Great Commission to "make disciples of all the nations"? Here are some ideas!

- Build a strong relationship with God through Bible reading and prayer.
- Make God the most important thing in your life so others will see his love in what you do and say.
- Use your gifts and talents to share about Jesus when he gives you the opportunity.

The Long-Awaited Transformation

The book of Genesis tells us about Eden, the beautiful garden where Adam and Eve lived—until they disobeyed God, causing sin to enter the world.

Because of the problem of sin, all creation has needed a transformation ever since. The Bible promises us that someday Jesus will return. He will change our world into a perfect place without any evil, pain, or death. The book of Revelation shares a spectacular vision that God gave to the disciple John. This vision describes what the new heaven and new earth will be like.

The new earth will be filled with light—there will be no more darkness and nothing to be afraid of. The light will not come from the sun or stars; it will come from God himself. In the new creation, God will live with his people, and they will see him face-to-face!

The new earth will also have a flowing river and a tree of life on each side of it. Back in Genesis, Adam and Eve were forced to leave the tree of life after they sinned. But guess what? In the new earth, everyone will get to eat fruit from the tree! In fact, the tree of life will produce a fresh crop of fruit each month. God will never stop providing for his people.

At the end of Revelation, John writes, "Come, Lord Jesus!" (Revelation 22:20). We can pray the same thing—that Jesus will come back soon, making everything right.

Guide to Following Jesus

Read the Bible
The Bible is God's Word. It's filled with amazing stories, wise words, teachings from Jesus, and more. The Bible is the ultimate source of truth, and it can guide you each and every day.

Pray
Prayer is simply talking to God. You can pray anytime, anywhere, and about anything. When you pray, you can praise God, ask him for help, confess your sins and ask forgiveness, and thank God for everything he's done for you.

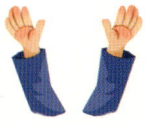
Worship
You can worship God in all sorts of ways. Here are some to try: sing songs of praise, go outside and thank God for his creation, or read the Bible and think deeply about God and his Word.

Connect
Spend time with other people who follow Jesus! You can ask each other questions, read the Bible together, pray as a group, and have fun with each other. If you don't have any Jesus-following friends, ask God to bring them into your life.

Serve
Jesus gave many examples of what it looks like to serve others. Did you know helping people can actually change you, too? As you help others, you'll become more like Jesus, and you'll learn to love them the way he does.

How to Lead Others to Jesus

Following Jesus is the best decision you—or anyone—could ever make! So what about the people in your life who haven't chosen to ask Jesus to be their Leader and Savior yet?

You can help others make the decision to follow Jesus too! In fact, Jesus tells all his followers to share about him with other people (see Matthew 28:19-20). He calls us all to tell people what he has done for us—how he loves and forgives us—and what he can do for them also.

Do you have a friend or family member who might want to know more about following Jesus? It can be scary to talk about your faith sometimes, so here are some steps to get you started.

1. **Pray.** Before you do anything else, pray for the person who doesn't know Jesus. God can give you courage to talk with them, and he can also help you know the right time to do so. God loves this person even more than you do!

2. **Share your story.** One great way to begin a conversation about Jesus is to share what he's done for you. Can you think of a time Jesus helped you with something or answered a prayer? What has changed in your life since you started following Jesus? What's your favorite thing about being a Jesus follower? The answers to these questions are good starting points for sharing your faith.

3. **Be a good listener.** A lot of people have questions about Jesus and about becoming a Christian. It's okay if you don't know all the answers! Being a good listener will show the person you care, and you can always ask a Christian adult about the answers later.

4. **Share what it means to follow Jesus.** Tell the other person that Jesus is the only one who can forgive our sins and transform our lives! Romans 10:9 says, "If you openly declare that Jesus is Lord and believe in your heart that God raised him from the dead, you will be saved." If the person wants to become a follower of Jesus, you can help them tell Jesus that they believe in him and want him to forgive and lead them. Jesus always says yes to that prayer!

5. **Invite them to church or Sunday school, and tell a Christian adult you trust.** It's wonderful when someone starts following Jesus, but they probably still have a lot to learn. That's why it's important for them to spend time with other Christians and start going to church. A Christian adult can help you invite them—and can pray for them with you.